P9-DCV-753

Build your own app

For Fun and Profit

Senior High School Library
Chippewa Falls, Wisconsin

Build your own app

For Fun and Profit

Scott La Counte ▶

an imprint of the American Library Association

HURON STREET PRESS

CHICAGO • 2012

Scott La Counte is a librarian at the Anaheim (CA) Public Library. He is the author of the book *Quiet, Please: Dispatches from a Public Librarian* (Da Capo Press, 2008), which began as a series for McSweeney's Internet Tendencies. He teaches writing online for the Gotham Writers' Workshops. He is also currently in charge of app development at Minute Help Press.

© 2012 by the American Library Association. Any claim of copyright is subject to applicable limitations and exceptions, such as rights of fair use and library copying pursuant to Sections 107 and 108 of the U.S. Copyright Act. No copyright is claimed for content in the public domain, such as works of the U.S. government.

Printed in the United States of America
16 15 14 13 12 5 4 3 2 1

Extensive effort has gone into ensuring the reliability of the information in this book; however, the publisher makes no warranty, express or implied, with respect to the material contained herein.

ISBNs: 978-1-937589-04-2 (paper); 978-1-937589-14-1 (PDF); 978-1-937589-16-5 (ePub); 978-1-937589-15-8 (Kindle).

Library of Congress Cataloging-in-Publication Data
La Counte, Scott, 1978-
Build your own app for fun and profit / Scott La Counte.
p. cm.
Includes index.
Summary: "Aimed squarely at the entrepreneur who knows little about mobile applications but is eager to know more, this primer explains in simple language this fast-growing segment of the world economy. The burgeoning smartphone and tablet market presents opportunities and new income streams for enterprising business managers. Avoiding jargon and technical language, the basics of mobile web applications are explained, and practical advice about using open-access development tools such as PhoneGap are discussed. A sample app is developed through the course of the book, providing a handy model for the reader. Even rookie developers with no programming experience will be able to create effective mobile applications using this handy introduction to a thriving billion-dollar industry"-- *Provided by publisher.*
ISBN 978-1-937589-04-2 (pbk.) -- ISBN 978-1-937589-14-1 (pdf) --
ISBN 978-1-937589-15-8 (kindle) 1. Smartphones--Programming. 2. Applicaton software. 3. HTML (Document markup language) I. Title.
QA76.76.A65L32 2012
006.7'6—dc23

2012002404

Series book design by Casey Bayer.

♾ This paper meets the requirements of ANSI/NISO Z39.48-1992 (Permanence of Paper).

Contents

ONE

Before You Begin

Mobile App: A Definition ▶ ··

An *app*, short for *application*, is a piece of computer software intended to help the user perform specific tasks. A *mobile app* is a piece of application software created for use in mobile phones and other handheld devices. It's difficult to write about mobile devices because that phrase can mean so many things. When I say *mobile app*, does that refer to an app that runs on any phone? Or on a specific phone? Just to be clear, there are two types of cell phones:

> **Feature phone:** A feature phone is what the average person carries in his or her pocket. Although many feature phones are becoming more sophisticated, for the most part, feature phones are the more popular basic phones that you can buy. They make calls, they offer texting, and most can take pictures and have very limited web

browsing. More than 80 percent of Americans have a feature phone.

Smartphone: Smartphones are best described as computers in the palm of your hand. Several times more powerful than feature phones, smartphones not only can surf the Internet but also can surf at relatively fast, third/fourth-generation (3G or 4G) speeds. The iPhone, Android, BlackBerry, and Windows Mobile are all examples of this kind of phone.

Many of the ideas in this book are universal; they can be tried on pretty much any phone in existence; the majority of ideas, however, are maximized for use with smartphones.

What is the point of developing apps that fewer than 20 percent of the population can access? Smartphones are the future of cellular technology. Smartphone prices have dropped significantly in recent years. When the iPhone was released in 2007, it cost $599; less than five years later, it cost as little as $99. The same is true of BlackBerries and nearly all other smartphones. As costs continue to drop, the smartphone is becoming more and more affordable to the average consumer.

Mobile development has become one of the biggest growth sectors of web development. People still use computers to surf the Internet, but the amount of time they spend on a computer will decrease as other devices become more prevalent.

The advent of XHTML-MP (XHTML for the Mobile Phone) and WCSS (Wireless CSS) converted two of the most powerful tools in web design into forms that are suitable for those who need to build mobile websites, that is, websites that are specifically designed to be viewed *only* on mobile phones and not computers. At the same time, WYSIWYG (what you see is what you get) editors currently provide templates for mobile websites, which makes it possible for just about anyone to design simple websites.

Perhaps the biggest reason businesses and other organizations need to embrace this growing technology is because the youth of the world use it to speak to one another. The average teen, if given the option, would probably prefer to text a person than to visit them in person or even call them. If your company is going to continue to grow, then now is the time to start considering the trends of our youth—the rapid growth of SmartPhones has proven this trend is not turning into a dying fad. When people buy phones, they are starting to expect apps, and when they don't see them, then they might just go to the company that does. Apps don't have to be flashy, at least right now; being able to tell your customer "I see you have an iPhone—make sure and download our app. It's free and tells you a little more about our company" is enough to give them the impression that your company is one that values technology.

The beauty of apps is that they are always evolving—there's plenty of time to grow the app into something that is truly eye-catching; if you can at least get something basic on Apple's app store (the online marketplace on which iPhone and iPad apps are sold), however, you'll have the competitive edge. For many customers, the app store is becoming more and more like the yellow pages. Need to buy a house? Go to the app marketplace to see what's available. More and more people are finding businesses through the app marketplace than the traditional phone directory. For some businesses, a top-rank match on the app marketplace will lead to ten times more customers than being the first name that pops up in a phone directory.

There are hundreds of thousands of apps, which sounds intimidating—until you consider the percentage of these apps that are merely games, fart sound effects, or big corporations like Disney,

NBC, and CNN. The percentage of smaller businesses that have apps is next to nothing—meaning in almost every sector, you can get there before your competition does. Don't be intimidated by the numbers—there is still plenty of room and plenty of opportunity to get the competitive edge over other businesses.

What Is a Mobile App? ▸

Another question that should be answered before proceeding any further is, What do I mean by "mobile app"? Mobile apps generally refer to two different things:

Mobile website: A mobile website is mobile phone-friendly and is developed taking into consideration the limitations of cellular devices. If you invested the right amount of time in your business's website, it probably looks pretty good on a ten- to twenty-inch screen (the size of the average desktop or laptop screen). But if you try to access the website from a mobile phone, it probably will look pretty lousy—if it even loads at all. Having a mobile-friendly website would simply mean that the business has a separate web address (e.g., m.business .com—the *m* standing for mobile) to point mobile phones to. This can be done easily by inserting code that redirects the device on the basis of its resolution. For example, if the site detects a device resolution of 1280 × 1024, then it's obviously a desktop, laptop, or tablet computer, and so would be directed to the main page; if the resolution is 320 × 480 or less, then it's some sort of mobile device, and so would be directed to a mobile page.

Native app: A native app is one for which the business has gone the extra step to create an app that is available for purchase in mobile app stores (e.g., iTunes, Android Market)

At the very least, every business should have a mobile-friendly website; it's a relatively easy process that I'll talk about in forthcoming chapters.

Developing a Mobile App ▶

Businesses that want to take the extra initiative and do something more innovative should devote some time to developing a plan for the delivery of native apps to their users. To develop a native app, you have to understand how to develop a mobile website app—so by understanding one, you are actually learning to do two things. By the end of this book, you might realize that you don't want to have a native app, but you will at least know how to develop one, and in doing so, you will be able to develop a mobile app.

The problem with developing a native app isn't the skill level (which is actually about the same as for developing a mobile-friendly website); the problem is the number of phones that are on the market. If you want to develop a native app for all users, then you have to develop one for every phone: iPhone, BlackBerry, Android, Palm, Windows Mobile—and those are just the major ones! In short, developing a native app requires a substantial time investment, and each business needs to consider that when deciding whether to invest in a native app.

The good news is that most phone makers supply app developers with plenty of free tools and resources to make development a little easier. The bad news is that actually getting the app into the mar- •

ketplace requires a bit of money; each phone requires that developers pay a fee, and some apps are compatible only with Mac operating systems, such as those for the iPhone. These costs, though, help prevent people who are not serious about app development from flooding the markets with apps. The box below illustrates the system requirements and fees for each of the five major phones. The information can be a little overwhelming, and chances are that you will not be able to get a business app on every phone. What you

---

System Requirements and Fees

Android
Fee: $25 unlimited
System requirements: The Android software development kit (SDK) is free. It requires
  ▸ Windows XP (32-bit) or Vista (32- or 64-bit)
  ▸ Mac OS X version 10.5.8 or later (x86 only)
  ▸ Linux (tested on Linux Ubuntu Hardy Heron)

BlackBerry
Fee: $200 for 10 app submissions
System requirements: The BlackBerry SDK is free. It requires
  ▸ Windows 2000 SPI or later, or Windows XP
  ▸ 32-bit Windows Vista (BlackBerry JDE v4.2.1 and higher)
  ▸ Java SE JDK v6.0

iPhone
Fee: $99 per year
System requirements: The iPhone SDK is free. It requires Mac OS X or later to run the program.

Palm
Fee: $99 per year
System requirements: The Palm SDK is free. It runs on Mac, Linux, and Windows.

Windows Mobile
Fee: $99 per year
System requirements: Windows XP or later with Visual Studio 2008 and Microsoft .NET Compact Framework v2 SP2.

need to consider, however, is that if you get a native app on just two phones (e.g., iPhone and Android), then it will be compatible with most smartphone users. In the summer of 2011, more than half of smartphone users are expected to have iPhones; Android is catching up quickly, with more than 30 percent of the market. That means that if ten people walk into a store to buy a smartphone, eight or nine will walk out with either an iPhone or a phone with the Android operating system.

The Essence of the Mobile Web ▸

Mobile websites should look and interact much differently than traditional websites. Mobile websites involve different design concerns than regular websites that you view on a computer. In some ways, designing mobile websites is like designing sites in the past, when the download speed of a page was of primary concern. Although today most mobile connections are quite fast, some mobile phone users pay by the minute for Internet connectivity; thus, it's in their best interest to access sites that download in short order.

All of this plays into simplicity, a major component of all good mobile websites. Regular websites offer a host of options to visitors, as well as graphics, images, navigation menus, Flash elements, and JavaScript elements that add functionality and style to the page. But where mobile websites are concerned, the aesthetic elements have to work hand in hand with practical concerns. On a small screen, there's no room for overblown design elements, multiple navigation menus, or a great deal of text. Unlike regular websites, mobile sites also require that you accommodate the technology that users have to view them.

The language of the Web is HTML, or HyperText Markup Language. For older mobile browsers, the language is WML, or Wireless Markup Language. Today smartphones and mobile browsers generally make use of XHTML-MP. The differences between HTML and XHTML-MP aren't too radical, and anyone with HTML experience should be able to figure out XHTML-MP with little difficulty. There are other requirements that mobile websites have to accommodate to make sure that their elements display correctly on all of the many mobile browsers on the market. Some of the features they require are the following:

- very simplified navigation
- layouts specified using Cascading Style Sheets (CSS), not tables
- compact, efficiently written content
- a color scheme that is consistent across all browsers
- reduction in bandwidth-heavy elements, such as pictures, videos, and audio
- navigation options such as "back" and "next" on every page

Most mobile websites are built around a utilitarian aesthetic. They aren't the places to show off your design department's abilities or to debut new and untested features. When people surf the mobile-friendly Internet, they're generally looking to find the information they want as quickly as possible, and that information is usually not for pure entertainment. Efficiency is always the first order of business with mobile sites. For example, for business sites, most users will primarily want to get directions to different offices, and e-mail/phone numbers of employees—chances are they won't want to use their phone to do something complex, so it's perfectly acceptable to keep it basic. Most modern businesses have found success in making their company more personal—giving their company a voice; this can be done by something as simple as daily or weekly blogs that are fed into the app; if you have time, then a few

---

Dimensions in Pixels

- **iPhone:** 320 × 480
- **Blackberry:** 160 × 160 to 480 × 360
- **Android SDK:** 320 × 240 (because different phones use the Android platform, here the dimension is the standard resolution in the developer kit)
- **Generic Windows Mobile:** 240 × 320 (standard resolution, but varies from phone to phone)
- **Nokia:** 95 × 95 and higher (varies from phone to phone, but 240 × 320 is standard)
- **Palm Pre:** 320 × 480

---

videos of employees and the office environment can also give your company that friendly voice you want—and, again, these videos can be hosted off the app like blogs and fed into the app—that way you can update the videos without updating the app.

Another concern in developing mobile websites is space. A smartphone, useful as it is, has a small-format screen. This means that you must maximize the space available and not create a mobile site that is useful only to those users who have relatively large mobile screens.

It's also important to see the actual phones and know what they look like. The average phone has a screen dimension of 320 × 480 pixels (about the same as a playing card); ideally, that is the resolution that you should aim to develop your mobile website for.

Surveying Users ▶

Before you continue with developing an app, it's a good idea to understand who your clients are and what kinds of mobile services they want. For example, what percentage of clients have smartphones? What kinds of smartphones do they have? (Many people don't know which kind of phone they have, so it's a good idea to ask to see their phone.) If they don't have smartphones, do they use the Web on their feature phones? Most web analytics sites (e.g., Google Analytics, StatCounter) will indicate users' resolution, which lets you figure out whether they are using a phone to view the site. But this doesn't always help because these sites let you know only whether users are accessing the site via their phone, not what kind of phone (e.g., iPhone, BlackBerry, Droid) they are using.

A lot of this book focuses on the iPhone, because when people talk about wanting to learn how to make apps, they are usually referring to making them for the iPhone—the holy grail of app development. Depending on your clients, however, you might want to consider starting on another device. There is no point in developing an iPhone app if most of your smartphone-carrying patrons have BlackBerries.

If you decide to continue with developing an app, then you have to ask, what do your clients want? Knowing if something is in stock? Photos from events? A calendar of events? GPS tracking to find the nearest business site? Instant messaging with a business representative? It's important to consider that what the business finds important is not necessarily what clients find important.

Training Staff ▸

The business might face resistance early on from staff and/or your boss. Chances are the company has been run successfully for several years, so you are bound to face someone who asks you, "Why waste time and energy in something that's unproven when the company is running just fine?" If you are the boss, then it doesn't really matter what people think—but you still don't want to lose staff morale. That's why it's especially important to get everyone in as soon as possible and make them feel like they can contribute. The most important thing to point out to staff or company owners is that this is cheap, and this will not take that much time. Also, it helps to show, not tell. Basically, that means that it's better to show a scene than to simply talk about what is happening. So, if you simply tell staff what the business wants to do, many might not see the necessity of an app, but if you show them the app and what it can do for the business, they're more likely to get excited.

How do you show? The best way is to carry out a survey on an iPod Touch or Android tablet. SurveyMonkey and other popular online surveys are great tools for collecting data, but actually placing a device in the hand of a staff member unfamiliar with such devices will help him or her become more comfortable with using the interface. These devices are also small, so they're easy to store. And for surveying clients, you can buy an iPod lock (e.g., the Targus Defcon Notebook/iPod Lock Combo costs $39.99) or lock an iPod to an unattended desk for clients to fill out the survey.

The iPod and Android tablets also use the same kind of interface as the iPhone, and there are plenty of survey apps that you can purchase for them; best of all, they are relatively cheap (less than $200). The Samsung Galaxy and Dell Streak tablet have received a lot of media attention, but there are many other tablets available—there are many Android tablets available on eBay for less than $150.

You can use Survey on the Spot (free for iPhone) or Askdroid and ODK Collect (free for Android) to create a survey, and then have librarians use the app to ask patrons a series of questions. Or use Tally Counter (free for iPhone) or CodeArk Tally Counter (free for Android) to count the number of people using smartphones. More powerful (and detailed) tally counts are also available for a price: Tallymander ($3.99 for iPhone) and Advanced Tally Counter Pro ($0.99 for Android) lets users count several different stats at once (e.g., types of questions patrons ask at the reference desk).

The results of the surveys, in most cases, won't be as powerful or specific as those you would get from sites like SurveyMonkey, but that doesn't matter; what matters is your letting people who don't regularly use the device know what it is. Even though people might resist change, almost everyone loves to play with gadgets!

Many times businesses implement technological innovations that don't take off because the staff members don't promote them to clients. But in surveying staff and patrons on an iPhone or tablet, even though you might not convert anyone to a smartphone user, you will at least give people a better understanding of their importance.

TWO

Developing a Mobile Web Application

Once you know who your users are, it's time to start developing. This chapter and the following ones provide a crash course in mobile development. We'll review the essence of HTML, CSS, and JavaScript programming, and we'll learn the very basics of what it takes to develop a mobile website.

Setting Up the Domain ▸

Mobile websites are housed in a separate part of your server from your main site. In most cases, the site name will simply have "mobile" added on at the beginning of the domain. For example, the mobile version of the URL YourBusiness.com would be Mobile .YourBusiness.com. The "Mobile" directory holds all the files required to display your mobile site. This type of organization also makes things easier on your information technology staff, because the "Mobile" directory is a convenient way to deal with a site.

Once your domain is set up and ready to go, the hard work begins.

Understanding the Process ▸

Most of the process of designing a mobile website involves simplifying and reformatting the information and features that appear on your main website. This means that, to build a mobile website, you first need to prepare the text and images for the site so that they fit the site's format.

Mobile Web versus Standard Web ▸

Everything on your mobile website will be slightly different from how it appears on your regular website. This is inevitable. Although there are some features that your users will expect from your website, some of what you offer on your main site is impractical for mobile users. It's important to remember that you're trying to replicate the functionality and content of your regular website as much as possible on your mobile site. You're not simply duplicating your main website and putting it in your mobile directory.

Your mobile website, therefore, should largely be its own entity—it will have some features from your main site, but you'll abandon others. You can start building your mobile site by streamlining your regular website.

Navigation ▸ ···

Most websites feature navigation menus with many options on the side or top of the page. For mobile sites, you'll need to reduce the number of navigation elements down to those that are the most practical and necessary for the patrons visiting your site. You will also want to add a "Back" and "Forward" button on every page. Some mobile browsers don't have these buttons built in, so it's easy for surfers to end up at a dead end on the site, which can be extremely frustrating.

The first thing that should appear on your mobile home page is the name of your business and your location(s). Your telephone number should also be one of the first pieces of information that your visitors see. Many visitors to your mobile website will simply opt to call and ask their questions directly to a staff member. You can make this easy for them by inserting a link that allows visitors to dial your phone number directly from the page. To insert the link, which should appear at the very top of the page, there is a fairly simple code that will display your phone number and allow visitors to dial the business just by clicking on the link:

```
<p align="center">Call Us:
<a href="wtai://wp/mc;5555551212">555-555-1212</a><br/>
<a href="wtai://wp/ap;5555551212;City_Business">Add Us to
Your Phone Book!</a>
</p>
```

By clicking on "Call Us," customers can dial the number listed. Notice that the unformatted phone number appears at the end of the line that starts "wtai" in both cases. In the second link, "Add Us to Your Phone Book!" the tag "City_Business" determines how your number will be added to the user's phone book. Providing the ability to both dial your phone number right from the mobile home page and add your number to the visitor's phone book with just a click is a huge convenience for your customers—and it definitely has a wow factor. One very easy way to get this same trick to apply to mapping your company's physical address is going to Google Maps (www.google.com/maps), typing in your company's address, and hitting search; this will pinpoint your company's address on a map, and on the left side you see the address with a hyperlink— right click that and select "Copy Link Address." Now you have an address to the map, so you can add a link that just says "Click for Address" and hyperlink it to the link that you copied.

Navigation buttons on a mobile website need to be very simple. In most cases, users prefer to move through your site using navigation menus. Entering text is difficult on some phones and, therefore, users tend to avoid doing so whenever possible. Also, your navigation choices should be intuitive, and ideally, it should take a minimal amount of clicks for patrons to find the page they're looking for.

Keep the shapes of your navigation buttons as simple as possible and use fonts that are bold and readable. Some mobile screens have very low-quality graphics, so make efforts to accommodate users of those devices when you're designing your site. For example, text links are preferable to graphics links.

The home pages of some mobile websites are little more than a small section of information with links provided underneath the main content. For examples of the effective use of this design, take a look at the mobile websites of some of the larger retailers—many of them follow this design.

For businesses, it also makes sense to organize navigation menus following the conventions for organizing books. For example, if clients can browse the catalog on the site, then a person trying to find a granite tile might follow the navigation series "G_Gr-Gt_ Tile" to find the desired records. Each element of this navigation could be a different button—"G," "Gr-Gt," "Granite Tile"—which would allow users to easily reach their destination without typing anything into the interface.

You can also use header tags to make your content easy to navigate. Headers are preferable to long text blocks on mobile websites. For instance, convert options such as

```
<p>You can browse our catalog by clicking below</p>
```

to

```
<h1>Browse Catalog</h1>
```

Content ▶ ⋯⋯⋯⋯⋯⋯⋯⋯⋯⋯⋯⋯⋯⋯⋯⋯⋯

The content for mobile websites needs to be much different from that of standard websites. For example, the content on mobile websites should be much briefer than on standard sites. Think about it like this: a mobile website page is to a normal website page what a card catalog record is to the book it represents. Your mobile pages have to be designed for people who are surfing for different reasons but whom you can cater to in the same fashion.

Most of the users of a businesses mobile site will seek out very specific information. It doesn't matter what they're doing at the time that they're browsing. They might be running errands, or they might be sitting in a coffee shop in no particular rush. Both kinds of users, however, want to be able to find what they're looking for in a reasonable amount of time. This means that content on a mobile site can be drastically cut back in comparison to that of a regular website.

The home page of a regular website often contains news, notices of updated pages, and much more. Some contain an "About Us" statement or other public relations information. None of this is really necessary on a mobile website. Regular websites are designed to be something of an experience in and of themselves, but mobile sites wow users with their functionality.

So, in designing your mobile site, reduce your content to the bare minimum. You can even probably eliminate altogether most of the material about your organization that appears on the home page of your regular website.

Formatting Content ▶

Even though small screen sizes are always a concern with mobile websites, there are several larger screen resolutions in use among smartphones. Some of them are more common than others. At the smallest end, 128 × 160 is fairly common. This screen size applies for most of the cheaper phones on the market. At the high end, 320 × 480 is fairly common among newer-model smartphones and other more sophisticated mobile devices. These screens are of different shapes, which makes it difficult to predict the look of a given mobile website on any particular phone. Designers have ways of getting around this, though, and many companies offer several websites—one for standard computers, one for smartphones, and one for feature phones.

Designs for mobile websites should incorporate many linear elements. Keep your lines simple and your design functional.

People using mobile devices with very small screens will have a hard time viewing a page that is crowded with large elements. If you position elements on your page on the basis of how they look on a specific device, you may be disappointed to find that the page looks much different when viewed on a different device. The more basic and linear the page design, the easier it will be for more of your visitors to use.

Remember that there is little flexibility in horizontal movement on mobile websites. You should orient your content so that users naturally move from the top to the bottom of the page.

Interactivity ▶

People using mobile devices generally aren't using a mouse. Instead of a mouse, however, smartphones have many different features that users can activate by tapping on the screen, and some of them have drag-and-drop functionality.

One of the conventions of web design is to avoid including elements that only users who have the most advanced equipment can access. In design parlance, this is sometimes called "accessibility." To make your site accessible to everyone, you should minimize the elements that depend on the user having touch-screen functionality.

For example, on navigation menus, most users will navigate with an "Up" and "Down" button to move from one option to the next. This means that some of the elements common to regular websites—drop-down menus, links in discrete areas of a site—are not always suitable for mobile websites. They can be downright frustrating to users whose devices don't allow for easy interaction with those particular elements.

Arrange navigation elements logically from the standpoint of someone using "Up" and "Down" buttons to move around the site. Doing so doesn't diminish the functionality of the site at all for users with more advanced devices, but it makes life much easier for those who have older phones.

If a lot of your users don't have or aren't likely to have newer mobile devices or smartphones, you might want to consider offering your mobile site in WML. Any mobile device can render pages written in this language. Not all older devices will be able to render the XHTML-MP elements that you may intend. One difference between mobile devices and personal computers, however, is that mobile devices tend to have shorter lifetimes and that people tend to upgrade them much more frequently than they do their computers.

Images ▶

Mobile devices, and especially the newer generation of smartphones, can accommodate images on their screens. All mobile devices have two characteristics, however, that make them inherently bad venues for large images and animations:

1. They have to accommodate very short download times.
2. The screen size makes viewing large images difficult.

As much as possible, eliminate images from your site. Then, you have to compress any images that remain, such as logos or banners. Both JPEG and GIF formats are excellent for mobile devices. As much as possible, however, your site should be text-based to optimize download times.

Bringing It All Together ▸ ·····································

Most WYSIWYG HTML editors today can accommodate mobile pages, and they usually include several different templates. Use one of these templates to lay out your site. You don't have to move beyond basic layout at this point, but concentrate on arranging things in logical order and, if you have a test server, test the site on different mobile devices.

It's vital at this point to make sure that your graphics display as intended and that your navigation menus are sensible and easy to move through on a mobile device. To add style to mobile websites, it's best to use CSS, which reduces the size of each page and allows you to change design elements across the whole site by altering only one file.

World Conference on Soft Computing ▸ ················

The World Conference of Soft Computing (WSC3) conventions on HTML design are very important when designing mobile sites as well. Check all of your code against the conventions to make sure it's valid. You can use online validators or the ones built into most of the commercially available WYSIWYG editors. Because of the tremendous variability in how a page displays from one phone to the next, it's important that your site operates as predictably as possible, and that means making sure that your code is valid.

THREE

Using CSS

This chapter is a crash course in Cascading Style Sheets, or CSS; if you already know how to use CSS, then this chapter will be a refresher. For a comprehensive view of CSS, I recommend that you check out *CSS: The Missing Manual,* by David McFarland (O'Reilly Media, 2006). What's important for you to know is that, although CSS is certainly useful and beneficial in developing a mobile website, it is not essential. If you don't use it, you can still develop a fully functional mobile website. So here are the basics.

The CSS tool was created to solve a specific problem with HTML, and it has since proved among the most useful of all Internet innovations. In HTML, every piece of text can have its properties specified individually. For example, you can specify that a certain line of text is red, underlined, and 12 points. If you want to, you can specify these properties separately for each letter on a page. This method, however, vastly increases the page's size and, more important, creates a lot of extra work for the designers, who have to specify each instance of how a link should look, how paragraph text should be displayed, and so forth. CSS eliminates this hassle.

A Cascading Style Sheet is really just a text file. It is usually separate from the main HTML code and, on the page, there is a call for that style sheet written into it that determines which style sheet will be used and, thus, how the page will look. Using CSS with mobile devices requires the inclusion of some tweaks to the code's language. This led to the development of Wireless CSS (or WCSS), which is tailored to mobile sites. If you understand CSS fairly well, you should have no trouble understanding WCSS.

To understand how CSS works, think of your website as consisting of two main parts. The first part is the content of the site, which is specified in the XHTML-MP document that you created on the basis of your HTML site. The second part of the site is the WCSS component, which determines how your site actually looks when it's displayed in a browser. With WCSS, you can also add some functionality and text effects.

How Powerful Is WCSS? ▸

WCSS is enormously powerful. Basically, one text file controls the entire look of your site, including every element on the page.

The syntax of CSS and WCSS is easy to understand. A selector identifies every element on your page that can be tagged with HTML (e.g., H1, P, A). These selectors have properties, such as color, size, ornamentation, and so forth, and all of those properties have values, such as red, 12 point, or underline. These properties are entered in a very simple format. For example, if you want every H1-level heading on your site to be green, the WCSS code is as follows:

```
h1 {color: green}
```

You can also use the number code (i.e., hexadecimal code) to specify color. For example, for all your paragraph text to be black, you would use the following code:

```
p {color: 000000}
```

You can use any HTML tag as a selector. To specify multiple properties for any given selector, separate them with a semicolon. In most cases, designers also place each property on a separate line, with the closing curly bracket on a line of its own. For example, for all paragraph text to be 8-point black, and specified as such in the style sheet, you would properly express it in the following way:

```
p
{
font-size: 8pt;
color: black;
}
```

This formatting of the text file does nothing to change how the WCSS renders your page. It does, however, make it easier for other designers to pick up your work and to see how you have set up everything—where mobile web pages are concerned, adhering to standards is vital.

Expanding the Flexibility ▸ ·······································

ID selectors allow you to be more specific about the look of your page. An ID selector refers to a single instance of an item. So, for example, if you want one specific text element to render differently than all others, you could specify it in the CSS by using the following line (for the purposes of example, we'll name this class "special"):

```
#special
{
color: orange;
}
```

Class tags allow you to specify this for an entire class of recurring elements on your page. For example, you could make all of the text that specifies business policy its own class and set it off in red as follows:

```
.policy
{
color: red;
}
```

The power in this is that you could change any property of every instance of the specified class, or type of text, with no more than a few keystrokes. This has some creative uses as well. For instance, for the Fourth of July, you can change your mobile site's color scheme to red, white, and blue; during Halloween, you can make it orange and black. You can make special style sheets and keep them on hand for various occasions, or you can revamp your website by changing just one file.

Using CSS Intelligently ▸

CSS is primarily useful because it reduces the amount of work it takes to develop and maintain a site by reducing the complexity of making changes across your entire website. To use CSS effectively, you need to keep your style sheets properly formatted and your classes and IDs limited to elements that merit those distinctions. For example, the more you separate common elements of your site into separate IDs and classes, the harder it will be to make large-scale changes. As much as possible, keep your site consistent with respect to the look of the headers and other elements; doing so will make it easier to make broad changes.

You can also use CSS to format links. This is a good way to reduce your site's dependency on graphics, because you can get rid of JavaScript rollover images and other resource-consuming elements that add little in the way of functionality. Simplifying your site with CSS can reduce page-load times; keep a consistent look throughout the pages; and make it easier to put new ideas into place when you want to change the site around a bit, whether those changes are permanent or temporary.

Browser Sizes, CSS, and Positioning ▸

You can use CSS to determine how all the elements on a web page are positioned in relation to one another, in relation to the corners

Senior High School Library
Chippewa Falls, Wisconsin

of the screen, and in other ways. Because of this, CSS more easily accommodates the needs of diverse visitors than HTML does.

CSS versus Tables ▸

One of the easiest ways to position elements on a page in HTML is to use tables. The use of tables dates back to when the language was first designed, and older pages tended to use tables heavily. However, the use of tables has several disadvantages for mobile websites.

Tables add information to the HTML page, as their dimensions and other properties have to be defined in the document. For mobile sites, reducing the size of files is paramount, and CSS allows for this by keeping that information in an external file, not in the document itself.

Tables are also clumsier with respect to laying out objects. When the specified dimensions of objects are too large to be accommodated by a specific screen, tables tend to crowd objects together or to bleed them off the side of the page. When objects are too small, tables waste valuable page space. In this regard, CSS offers superior positioning options.

Absolute Positioning ▸

Absolute positioning means specifying that elements of the page appear in specific areas of the screen, regardless of the screen size. Absolute positioning can be used to accommodate all users because the page elements display correctly on even the smallest of screens. A well-designed page will always look good on larger screens, but there will be more unused space on the display. The CSS for setting an element's position in absolute terms is written as follows:

```
h1
{
position:absolute;
left:25px;
top:50px;
}
```

This code tells the browser to display anything labeled <h1> at 25 pixels from the left of the screen and 50 pixels from the top. That way, no matter the user's screen size, the mobile device will display content tagged "h1" in that position.

Relative Positioning ▸

Relative positioning allows you to specify a container and position the page elements within that container. This type of positioning is sometimes used on sites to better control for smaller resolutions. For example, if you have a borderless background, you can frame your page within the confines of an 800 × 600 monitor resolution and position all the elements on your page within that container.

Floating ▸

Most web designers use floating to position elements, as this simply places elements preferentially to the right or the left of the screen. If there isn't room to accommodate the elements on the screen, then they can appear in a logical order that flows from top to bottom. This accommodates the linear design requirements of mobile websites, which makes this method very convenient.

Making Your First CSS Document ▸ ·······························

All you need to make a CSS document is a text editor. The selectors, their properties, and their property values are expressed as detailed above, and there is little complexity to deal with.

Embedded style sheets appear at the top of the document, within the header. To change any given page that uses such a style sheet, you must change each style sheet individually.

Linked style sheets are stored in a separate file, which offers the most convenience when you need to make massive changes to a site. Your style sheet is called for in the header of your document. The tag looks like this:

```
<link rel="stylesheet" type="text/css" href="your_style_sheet_
here.css" media="all">
```

If you're creating a style sheet manually, simply give it a name and save it in a directory in your website. In the header of your web page, paste in the previous tag. This will link the page to the style sheet, and the style sheet will then determine the look of the page. If you want to change the look of the page, simply specify a different style sheet in the link.

Keeping It Simple ▸ ....

Remember that mobile devices have considerably less display area than computers. When you start putting together the layout of your site, keep it very simple.

A popular page design makes use of three elements that allow users to make the most of the mobile presence:

1. A banner with a phone number
2. Text links to other pages
3. A search field

For most businesses, these three elements make for an excellent home page. There are few elements to arrange and, as long as the elements are designed with forethought and correctly positioned, they should display effectively in every mobile web browser. Because there is so little on the page, it will also load quickly. You can even eliminate the graphic for the business logo altogether and replace it with a simple text link. This makes the site more accommodating for those who have older-generation mobile devices. On a feature phone you are most worried with presence, not branding; you just want to get them into your business. Having the company's logo may actually push the content that's important further down and make the user work hard to find what they are looking for; you want your app to be as convenient and easy to navigate as possible.

Remember that the more your navigation relies on simple text links, the less space you will lose to graphics. Of course, you can use CSS to make elegant text links, including ones that provide rollover effects and other visually interesting elements—this is yet another reason to employ the CSS tool whenever possible.

If you want to add graphical menus and other functionalities to your mobile site, you'll need to learn a bit about JavaScript, which is a ubiquitous web language. However, it is also complex and takes a qualified programmer to write it. Understanding how JavaScript works and what it offers, however, is the last step in determining how to put together your page.

FOUR

JavaScript and Mobile Website Design

This chapter is meant to give you an overview of what Java-Script is and how it functions—not to teach you everything you need to know; Danny Goodman's *JavaScript Bible* (Wiley, 2010) is the most comprehensive book you'll find on the subject. As with CSS, JavaScript isn't required for developing a mobile app, and it is less essential to designing a good app.

JavaScript is a client-side scripting language that allows users' computers to execute specific functions. In a less technical sense, JavaScript tells a device to perform various tasks. For example, some search pages automatically place your cursor in the search field for you. The cursor doesn't go there on its own; the site often uses JavaScript to place the cursor there.

JavaScript does not actually contribute a great deal to the layout of your page. There are no websites, mobile or otherwise, that are built on JavaScript alone. It is, however, an important element for adding functionality to your site, and to some extent, it can add some visual appeal.

Getting JavaScript ▸

JavaScript is extremely popular with both designers and programmers of regular websites. The reason for this is the power that it allows designers to wield over the functionality of their pages. In addition, using tools such as these can cut costs considerably. For example, JavaScript allows coders to use a much better known and more frequently used code without taking the time to learn a phones-native language to do essentially the same thing.

You can download libraries of various JavaScript resources and include them in your site, which is often easy to do and doesn't take any real programming knowledge. Usually, you only need to add a small script into the web page.

For mobile sites, though, JavaScript brings up some significant compatibility issues. Moreover, by adding code directly to your page, you increase its size. For users with browsers that lack JavaScript compatibility, that amounts to downloading extra data that offer no benefit at all.

The Basics of Including JavaScript ▸

Although you can add more advanced features with JavaScript, its support among mobile devices is spotty at best, and you should test it thoroughly before deploying the site.

JavaScript is a scripting language that works on any computer. It is included in the HTML of a page and allows browsers to perform a variety of functions. The code appears in the following format:

```
<script type="text/javascript">
document.write('Your message here!'); </script>
```

In the context of a full page, the script would be expressed in the following way:

```
<html>
<head>
</head>
<body>
<script type="text/javascript">
document.write('Your message here!');
</script>
<noscript>
Your browser either does not support JavaScript, or you have
JavaScript turned off.
</noscript>
</body>
</html>
```

This script would tell the browser to write "Your message here!" on the page in the position determined by the script's location in the HTML. You can specify the font and other attributes of the text, just as you can for any other element on an HTML page. JavaScript can get very complex, though, and some large scripts constitute large parts of the content of some web pages.

In the event that the visitor's browser doesn't support JavaScript, the site visitor would receive the message "Your browser either does not support JavaScript, or you have JavaScript turned off."

Some scripts are contained in the header of the HTML document and are called at the point in the body where their output is desired by a second code. These scripts can perform functions such as displaying dynamic information, providing messages based on user actions, or date and time. They can also be used to process some types of information and to perform simple functions. JavaScript can be custom coded, but even professional designers tend to make heavy use of the free libraries available on the Web, as those resources address the most common JavaScript issues.

JavaScript also is used in some cases to provide better accessibility to web page content, such as allowing users to make the page's text bigger.

JavaScript and Forms ▸ ···

JavaScript is used heavily for the handling of forms. For retailers, these might be forms that allow users to do a quick search of the site or of the product inventory, or to update their customer account information. There's no reason that you can't provide these functions on a mobile site; to perform them, however, the user has to provide you with specific information. This can be more resource-intensive than it sounds.

If a user submits a form with missing information to the server, the server has to process the form, figure out what's missing, and send it back to the user with the missing elements indicated. For mobile users, this can use up their airtime as they wait for all this to happen. JavaScript can inspect a form as it is filled out and, if there is something wrong, point that out to the user before they send it. This saves them time and saves your server's resources.

The drawback of using JavaScript is that many mobile web browsers do not support it at all. Therefore, adding JavaScript to your pages benefits only some users and may make the site work more poorly for the rest of them. So, designing with JavaScript is all about using it intelligently.

Where to Use JavaScript ▸ ···

If accessibility is an issue for your business, then you should have a version of your mobile website that does not employ JavaScript at all. Older phones often cannot execute JavaScript, which will make some of your site's features unavailable to some users. It's probably the case, though, that most users are using newer-generation phones.

On newer-generation phones, there are several ways you can enhance their experience on your site. For example, you can add code to your site that will detect the size of users' screens and change the style sheet used to render the site accordingly. This means that you can have a developed, ornate version of your site for the smartphone crowd and a simpler version for those using older phones. Combined with CSS, JavaScript can greatly increase accessibility in this way.

The way this works is fairly complex, but the overall concept is easy to understand. Whenever a mobile device visits your website, you can query as to what kind of device it is. When the information is sent back to the server, the server looks up the device on a list of mobile devices and matches it to the right phone on the basis of the dimensions of the screen. The phone information returned includes the screen dimensions, which the server then uses to send users the right web page for those dimensions.

JavaScript is often used to make pop-up windows—the useful kind, not the kind that was the source of much irritation in the past—animated menus, and other features that add visual interest to the page. On mobile sites, these things are best avoided, mostly because users navigate mobile websites differently than they do regular websites.

If you have different versions of your website for different devices, then you can offer some JavaScript functionality for those devices that can run it. This can make sure that devices that cannot process JavaScript do not receive versions of your page that are unusable.

Mobile devices are increasingly making use of nearly full-fledged browsers rather than specific apps for surfing the Web. This means that support for JavaScript among mobile browsers is increasing, and it will likely become a more common element in mobile web design.

Setting up a JavaScript element to detect smartphones can be useful, but it might not always work out as you plan. Some mobile browsers don't identify themselves correctly or are set up to identify themselves as a different type of browser, such as Internet Explorer. In addition, not everyone with mobile devices that support JavaScript will have the right feature turned on. In some cases, users block JavaScript altogether to enable faster page-load times and to keep their browsers more secure. These are all considerations when designing with JavaScript.

JavaScript Missteps ▸

One of the most popular uses of JavaScript is to create menus. In some cases, menus can be confusing to users. Users on mobile devices tend to navigate with buttons, not a mouse, so that's another reason to avoid going overboard with menus. For mobile devices, you should avoid rollover mouse effects (e.g., a button lights up or shifts position when you roll the cursor over it). On mobile devices, such menus require too much code and too many resources.

It's also important to make sure that your JavaScript applications are compatible with mobile devices. For example, not all mobile devices might have a substitute for the mouse, which means that the device might ignore altogether any events that are linked to the mouse, which may cause problems with the page. There are variations on JavaScript cursor actions designed to accommodate smartphones, but they are not universal. For example, the current generation of smartphones does not reliably support the drag-and-drop functionality that you can add to web pages with JavaScript.

There is expanding support for more mobile browsers, however. Free JavaScript libraries have more and more features with every revision that can provide added functionalities to smartphone browsers. Some of the newest innovations include the following:

▶ increasing support for touch screens
▶ support for scroll bars being placed within browsers
▶ support for more sophisticated animation

Because there is so much variation among mobile devices, however, there is still great inconsistency in JavaScript compatibility.

JavaScript Applications ▶

JavaScript is oftentimes used to create browser-based applications, such as measurement converters and simple games. However, these applications can become very complex, especially on very developed websites that offer a great deal of user functionality.

On mobile websites, applications can be a problem because of compatibility issues. Although they're great for incorporating into your main website, the mobile versions of most major websites eliminate JavaScript applications altogether. The potential benefits of using complex JavaScript applications are simply not reliably delivered even by the most advanced smartphones, although compatibility is sure to increase with time.

Is It Viable? ▸

Presently, mobile devices do not universally support JavaScript. This means that, in terms of accessibility, a business would have to offer a JavaScript-free version of any page it currently publishes on its website to enable the widest variety of users to access it. Functions that are completely dependent on JavaScript will not be available to those whose phones cannot support it. Some phones do support JavaScript, but it may not function as intended, particularly for user-action-triggered events, such as mouse-overs and hovers. This may make JavaScript unsuitable for some libraries and for the majority of their patrons.

However, you can use JavaScript in limited deployments and offer your visitors increased functionality and more convenience, especially in handling forms and other basic needs.

You can quite easily and inexpensively test JavaScript's suitability on your website. Because of the many free JavaScript libraries available and because anyone who can edit HTML can install the scripts on a page quite easily, you can check to see whether adding a feature based on JavaScript provides a better experience for your clients. Make sure you test it yourself on various devices: smartphones use different browsers, so check the functionality of your page on all smartphones.

Again, the most important element of mobile web design is simplicity. However advanced and developed your main site is, you'll have to strip it down to the essentials to make it useful for those who prefer to access it on the go. In some ways, your mobile site mirrors what you have on your main site, but it is better thought of as a separate entity altogether. It might contain a great deal of the same content as your main site, but it will be directed toward providing the fastest, most efficient, and most no-nonsense user experience possible. However, as mobile web use rapidly increases, there will be a significantly increased demand among business users to have business resources available on mobile devices.

Where Can Businesses Use JavaScript? ▸

If you are trying to decide whether you should learn JavaScript, you first need to ask how the business can use it. Two common uses for JavaScript is in developing forms and providing a chat-based service. It also is nice to have a place for customers to add and send comments, or to create a form page where customers can order something from their phone, or to find out if items are available, or to create a mobile-friendly inventory. But whether it's worth the time to learn the language is up to you. For chat-based services especially, there are relatively cheap non-JavaScript options as well, so it might be in your interest to use one of those services and save yourself the trouble of learning the language. If you don't already know Java programming, then you will probably be better off designing an app without it and looking into adding in JavaScript to the app later.

FIVE

PhoneGap

I decided that I was going to develop an iPhone app several months ago. It was the latest way to make money, so I figured, why don't I jump on the bandwagon? I checked out some books on iPhone development and watched a few YouTube videos. After about ten hours of research, the furthest I was able to get was to download the iPhone SDK. I've had my share of programming courses in college, and I was developing websites before most people even had computers with modems. I say this so you understand just how complicated programming apps can be.

I'm not an expert in programming language; I understand the theories behind it, but I know little about how to actually write code. When mobile development was just getting started, I was out of luck. However, a relatively new program called PhoneGap is helping bridge the divide for people with no or limited programming skills.

PhoneGap got started in 2009 at the iPhoneDevCamp. The program allows developers to create a page like they would for the mobile Web—with HTML, CSS, and JavaScript—and quickly convert it to a language that's supported as a native app. Although PhoneGap is simple enough for anyone to use, companies like Wine.com have successfully built powerful apps with its framework.

The best thing about PhoneGap is that it's free and open source. But regardless of whether you will develop a mobile app, PhoneGap is a valuable resource if only because it has simulators to let you see what a website looks like on a particular phone without actually having the phone.

It's worth noting that, at the time of this writing, PhoneGap was bought by Adobe. One can only predict what they will do with the app and if they will ultimately charge for it. It is to their benefit, however, to keep it free and open source, giving companies an easy way to convert pages into apps without using the thing that Apple has an open vendetta against: Flash! In any scenario, the old version should remain available under free license but official support may (or may not) go away.

PhoneGap Features ▸

So, exactly what does PhoneGap do? In short, the PhoneGap software helps you turn a website into a mobile app. In theory, instead of learning several different mobile programming languages, you only need to know HTML. In practice, it's best to also know CSS and JavaScript, but knowing HTML will get you started.

PhoneGap also lets you take advantage of the features of individual cell phones (e.g., geolocation, accelerometer). Table 5.1 shows a list of all supported features of PhoneGap.

TABLE 5.1 ▸ **Supported Features of PhoneGap**

	iPhone	Android	Blackberry	Symbian	Palm
Geolocation	•	•	•	•	•
Vibration	•	•	•	•	•
Accelerometer	•	•	OS 4.7	•	•
Sound	•	•	•	•	•
Contact support	•	•	•	•	
Camera	•	•	•	•	
Multitouch	•	•			
Copy and paste		•			

What follows is a brief explanation of the PhoneGap features and examples of how they work in practice.

Geolocation: Geolocation is a feature in every newer-generation smartphone that enables the phone to use its internal GPS to determine its real-time location. What does that mean for an app? It could, for instance, let customers find out where the business is located in relation to their own position and help them get directions.

Vibration: Vibration lets you take advantage of the internal vibration setting available on phones. For example, developers could create an app that notifies users of alerts through vibration.

Accelerometer: An accelerometer is a feature first made popular by the iPhone but now available in nearly all phones. This feature rotates the screen when the phone is turned on its side.

Camera: All camera phones are built differently, and using the camera feature will likely result in some glitches.

A complete list of PhoneGap's features can be found online (http://wiki.phonegap.com/Roadmap); the site is updated often and includes extra documents and discussions where developers can find support.

Viewing Your Website on PhoneGap ▸ ....

Now it's time to see how your business's website looks on a mobile device. If you have a mobile phone, then this is easy; but just because your website looks great on Android doesn't mean that it will look equally great on an iPhone or a BlackBerry.

Figures 5.1 and 5.2 show two websites from the *New York Times*; figure 5.1 shows how the site looks on the iPod and iPhone as a regular site (not a mobile one); it's nearly impossible to read without zooming in, which isn't always practical for every user. Figure 5.2 is the *New York Times* mobile site, which is much easier to read on a smaller screen.

Figure 5.1   **Figure 5.2**

You want to know what your mobile site looks like on every phone imaginable. PhoneGap makes this easy; it has cell phone skins for testing websites on nine different phones (iPhone, Android G1, Blackberry Storm, Blackberry Bold, Palm Pre, Nokia N97, Samsung Epix, Sony Ericsson Satio, Sony Ericsson Rachael).

To test a website, run the PhoneGap Simulator (www.phonegap .com/tools/). When the Debug Panel (shown in figure 5.3) appears, type in the website address in the address bar and then click the right-arrow button.

Figure 5.3

If you want to view the website using a different skin, then click once on Menu in the PhoneGap Debug Panel, select Skin, and pick the phone that you want to switch to (figure 5.4).

Figure 5.4

Redirecting to a Mobile Site ▸ ⋯⋯⋯⋯⋯⋯⋯⋯⋯⋯⋯⋯⋯⋯

If you decide to have a mobile version of your site, then you will have to decide how to get phone users to it. There are two ways. First, simply have two addresses that you give out: a computer address and a mobile address. You can tell your customer to add "m" to the address when accessing the site from a phone (e.g., m.business.com). Just as it's pretty common knowledge that .edu is an educational site and .gov is a government site, most users will associate m.business.com as a mobile site, so it's really to the company's advantage to assign that "m" to the mobile page.

The second way is a little more difficult. It requires that you add code into your page that tells the page to search for the user's browser. If visitors to the website are using a mobile browser, then they will be redirected to the mobile-friendly site. Some websites, such as RottenTomatoes.com, have gone as far as directing users to download their iPad/iPhone app when they see that they are trying to get to the web page on that device—this, however, while simple for the user, requires hours of programming and is not best practice for simply setting up a mobile page quickly and easily. You need to understand PHP programming to implement such a task. You can also buy the code for $50 (http://detectmobilebrowsers. mobi/). *PHP and MySQL Web Development* by Luke Welling and Laura Thomson and *Learning PHP, MySQL, and JavaScript* by Robin Nixon are two fairly easy-to-understand books on the complex subject of PHP if you want to explore this further. For a great overview of how the process works, try out the tutorial "Apache 2: How to Redirect Users to Mobile or Normal Web Site Based on Device Using mod_rewrite" at www.howtoforge.com.

SIX

Building Your First Native App

Creating a Bare-Bones Native App ▸

This chapter will help you create a quick, bare-bones app that will run on the iPhone. I use the iPhone as an example because it is the device that most users will have for native apps—although Android is quickly catching up. The iPhone is also the easiest device to quickly develop apps for.

Despite some negative press about the iPhone app process being overly protective and the rejection of apps left and right, it is surprisingly easy and very friendly to use PhoneGap's open-source framework. As long as you adhere to the iPhone guidelines, which aren't as strict as they are sometimes made out to be, you will have no problem developing your app.

The first thing you need to do before you begin developing any app, be it mobile or web, is to draft a concept of what you want it

to include and look like. I recommend MockApp (www.mockapp
.com), a free service that lets you use PowerPoint to develop a sample iPhone app, one that you can run on your device as a PDF. It's
one thing to tell business administrators that the business needs an
iPhone app; it's another thing to show them what the app will look
like. Developing a sample app will let you quickly demonstrate
what the app will look like and how customers can take advantage
of its features. As you develop the app, keep in mind that you don't
want to have to update things too frequently.

Figure 6.1 shows the app that I developed for this book (it's
meant to look like an iPhone screen). The app is designed for a
library, but the template can be used for essentially any business,
local government office, or not-for-profit institution with very
minor tweaks. The code for the app appears at the end of this
chapter.

Unlike a mobile web app, for
which you have to be very care-
ful with images, native apps can
feature a few more graphics. All
of the images I used for this basic
app came from the Open Clip Art
Library (www.openclipart.org), a
great resource for businesses.

So let's talk about this app. All
the buttons are placed in what I con-
sidered the order of most importance
to library patrons. The most popular
buttons will likely be "Call the Business" and "Hours." This is what will
be the home screen.

Figure 6.1

Generic Business Logo: Whenever possible, I recommend
using the logo that patrons already know; try to also use
similar colors as on your main web page. Remember,
however, that users won't be normal computer users—
people who access the app are frequently outside and
their screen is harder to see. Colors are even more
important on a cell phone than on a computer.

Call: When creating apps there are two kinds of buttons; the
first is a hyperlink that takes you to another page. The
second is an action button. Action buttons do exactly
what the word *action* says. They might tell the phone
that the user wants to call a number; when pressed, the
phone automatically launches the dialer and begins to
make a call (see the end of this chapter for the code used
for the action button).

Hours: You can do one of two things with the "Hours" link:
you can create a mobile page with hours of operation,
which is the simplest and quickest approach, or you can
create a script that counts down the number of minutes
until the business either closes or reopens again.

Locations: Customers want to know not just where the
business is but also how to get there; this is where a
mobile app can help. To keep things simple, I won't go
into using GPS; if you want to know more, refer to the
PhoneGap website tutorial (http://docs.phonegap.com/
en/1.0.0/phonegap_geolocation_geolocation.md.html).
If the page no longer exists, Google "PhoneGap GPS"
and the first page that comes up from the PhoneGap.com
server will be the one you want.

Find a Product: Many businesses will be a little limited
in the "Find a Product" option. Here, however, is an

excellent place to simply showcase what you offer; maybe it's just a gallery of designer dresses that recently came in; or if you are a photographer, photos from weddings; the key in this section is simply to display your product—whatever it is.

Research via Local Library: Many research providers have yet to go mobile, so make sure you encourage them to do so. One vendor that has gone mobile is Gale, which has a terrific app called AccessMyLibrary. The app lets users use the database from their phone if they are within a ten-mile radius of the library—and no log-in is required. This means if you are a business near a library, you can promote this service to customers wanting to research products, and you don't have to pay a cent! This would be great for a day-care business that wants to point parents to well-researched articles on parenting techniques; a solar power company that wants to show its customers how solar panels can make their homes more efficient; even a beach shop that wants to show its potential customers why a certain sunscreen does a better job protecting their skin than others. Any business can benefit from this free resource!

Services: Obviously, you will want to reference the services you actually have in the business in this page; it is also possible, however, to put games on this page. If you are a business that has a children or teen audience, there are a number of places you can go to get JavaScript-based games that you could implement on these pages; a Google search will give you literally thousands of pages—some are open source, some are paid. JavaScript, especially on the iPhone, can be tricky; make sure you test the page to see if the JavaScript code actually works. When you are getting code from the Internet to use on a mobile app, it can be hit or miss. If you are a restaurant, you could put a PDF of your entire menu here—every SmartPhone now has PDF viewers built in. Later in the book, I will reference a few sites that help you create web apps, which can all be implemented here.

Videos: The next chapter goes into greater detail on this topic, but one thing to consider is providing videos of two- to three-minute demos of how to do different things on the computer—or even a hyperlink to a helpful YouTube video on different computer-related subjects. This could also provide how-to videos of different products you sell. If you have the time, a product commercial might also be beneficial—most phones (like the iPhone) make it incredibly simple to film, record, edit, and publish a video straight to YouTube—a computer isn't even required.

Text a Question: If you don't have a texting service at the business, get one! It's free! Google Voice is fine for most small firms. There's an easy code for an action button for this. Just add the following code to your app: <a href="sms:1234133424243">Text a Question</a>.

About: This is where you can explain the app's purpose and who to contact to report any bugs or glitches.

All the information on the app so far easily applies to web apps. Changing your app to an iPhone app requires only one or two extra steps.

The District of Columbia Public Library was one of the first public libraries to build an app for its book catalog; the library put the code for the app online, and it's free to copy (http://dclibrary labs.org/projects/iphone/). You may not want to use it (or may not even like it), but it's a good reference to start with as you begin to learn about code. If you are a business considering building your own inventory of goods (instead of outsourcing it), then this is an excellent resource.

Putting the App on the ▸ iPhone and iPod Touch

To begin installing your app on the iPhone, you will need to download both the iPhone SDK and PhoneGap (on an Intel-based Mac computer) from the following websites (Note: by the time of the publication of this book, there will be a newer version of the SDK, and some directions will look slightly different; Apple updates the SDK one to two times a year. PhoneGap does an excellent job of providing up-to-date tutorials weeks after the release of each new SDK):

> iPhone SDK: http://developer.apple.com/iphone/index
> .action/
> PhoneGap: www.phonegap.com

It's important that you save all of your mobile web files with the HTML extension (not HTM). If you have saved them as HTM, then make sure to rename them with the appropriate extension before proceeding. Also, make sure that your home page file is named "index.html."

Then move the mobile website you have created into the PhoneGap directory. After unzipping the PhoneGap files, open the PhoneGap directory and then open the iPhone directory (figure 6.2).

Figure 6.2

The iPhone app structure has already been created, so what you are doing at this point is simply applying your mobile web app to a prebuilt template. You can then drag and drop all of your mobile web app files into the WWW directory (figure 6.3).

Figure 6.3

Your first iPhone app is now complete! Yes, it really is that quick! There are still some tweaks left to perform, but the description here should give you a good idea of just how easy it is to get started developing apps for the iPhone.

To see your app in action, go back to the PhoneGap and iPhone directory and open the file "PhoneGap.xcodeproj." This will launch Xcode, the iPhone developer software (figure 6.4).

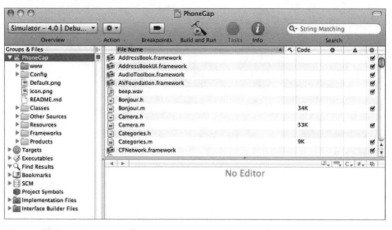

Figure 6.4

Next, click the drop-down menu in the upper-left corner of Xcode, make sure it is set to "Debug," and then select the simulator you want to run. It's best to select the most current simulator (iPhone 4.0), because that is the device that most people will have. It is also a good idea to ensure that the simulator runs on all platforms. For example, if you select iPad as your simulator, it will run the app as an iPhone app, not an iPad app, and so the app will appear significantly smaller than it would normally (figure 6.5).

Figure 6.5

You are now ready to build the app. Click the "Build and Run" button.

After about ten seconds the simulator will launch, and your app will appear. If it does not launch and you see red or yellow flags in the lower-right side of the screen, click on the flags to examine the message.

You will notice two things the first time the app loads. First, the icon is for PhoneGap; second, the loading image reads "PhoneGap." Let's see how to get rid of those two graphics and replace them with images.

Close the Xcode program and simulator.

Now, let's make an iPhone app icon. It's simple. Create an image with a dimension of 57 × 57; use the file name "icon.png" to save the image. Move the file you created into the PhoneGap and iPhone directory. The file will replace the already-created "icon.png" and replace it with your new one.

Next, let's change the start-up image. Repeat the steps to create an icon, except this time name your image "Default.png" and make sure it has the following dimensions: 320 × 480. Move this image into the PhoneGap and iPhone directory.

Before launching the Xcode app again, rename "PhoneGap .xcodeproj" to your actual app name; for our purposes, let's use "library.xcodeproj" as a file name. Once you rename it, open the file again, which will relaunch the Xcode software.

At this point, your icons and start-up screen will have changed, but the icon will still read "PhoneGap." To change the name that appears, click on the Config directory in the open window (figure 6.6).

Figure 6.6

This will bring up a new window at the lower-right side of the screen (figure 6.7). Under "Bundle display name," click on "PhoneGap" and then type in the name that you want to appear. For our purposes, I used the name "Library App."

Key	Value
▼ Information Property List	(14 items)
Localization native development re	en
Bundle display name	Library App
Executable file	${EXECUTABLE_NAME}
Icon file	icon.png
Bundle identifier	com.sintaxi.phonegapdemo
InfoDictionary version	6.0
Bundle name	${PRODUCT_NAME}
Bundle OS Type code	APPL

Figure 6.7

Before loading your app in the simulator again, go to the top of the screen, click on "Build," and then click on "Clean All Targets" (figure 6.8). It is advisable to do this before you run the simulator, just to make sure that you've saved and updated all changes.

Build	Run	Design	SCM	Window	⚡
Build Results				⇧⌘B	
Build				⌘B	
Build and Analyze				⇧⌘A	
Build and Archive					
Build and Run				⌘↵	
Build and Run – Breakpoints Off				⌘R	
Build and Debug – Breakpoints On				⌘Y	
Clean				⇧⌘K	
Clean All Targets					
Next Build Warning or Error				⌘=	
Previous Build Warning or Error				⌘+	
Compile				⌘K	
Preprocess					
Show Assembly Code					
Touch					

Figure 6.8

Finally, click on "Build and Run." Everything should now look as you want it to.

Moving Your App from the ▶ Simulator to the iPhone

To move the app from your computer to your iPhone or iPod for testing purposes (not to put it on the app store, which takes a little bit more work), you will need to obtain a provisioning profile for your app, for your device, and for yourself.

The first step is to go to the iOS Dev Center site (http://developer.apple.com/iphone/) to register to become a developer. Once you are logged in, you will see a menu bar on the right that reads "iPhone Developer Program" (figure 6.9).

Figure 6.9

Next, click on "iPhone Provisioning Profile." Then click on "App Ids" at the left-hand side; click on "New App ID" and fill in the information for your app.

Next click on "Provisioning" at the left side of the screen, and select "New Profile." Once you've created the profile, download it to your computer. In the next few steps, we will match the profile to the key that you'll generate for the iPhone or iPod that you wish to test the app on.

After you have created your provisioning profile, you'll want to return to the Xcode Organizer (located in the Window menu) to pull the product identifier from your device (figure 6.10). Once you've plugged in the device and opened the organizer, click on "Provisioning Profiles" and copy the app identifier. Next go back into Xcode, click on "Info.plist," and go to the box in the lower-right pane (figure 6.11). Change the bundle identifier to the one you have just copied, but leave in your user name.

Figure 6.10

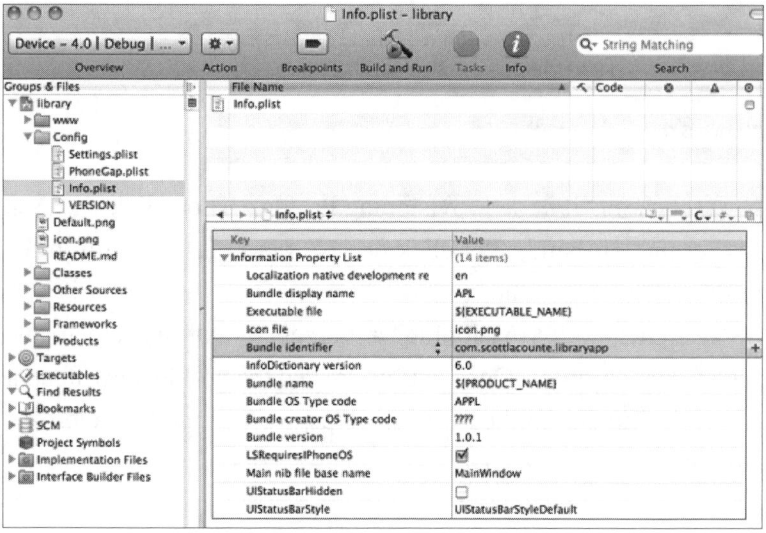

Figure 6.11

So your app ID should look something like this: IDNUMBER .com.scottlacounte.libraryapp (App ID.com.PROFILE NAME .APP NAME).

When you have installed all of the certificates and are finally read to go, the most important step is to make sure the Xcode is set to Device and not Simulator (figure 6.12). Until you switch this, the app will not load on the iPod or iPhone.

Figure 6.12

If you have done everything correctly, there will be a delay of approximately ten seconds before the iPod or iPhone turns on. If you missed a step, then in your device organizer there will be an orange circle next to the device (figure 6.13). When you click on the device, it will tell you what the error is. The most common error has to do with the provisioning profile not matching the device, which means that there is a certificate missing. Double-check the iOS Dev Center page to make sure you have downloaded all the certificates.

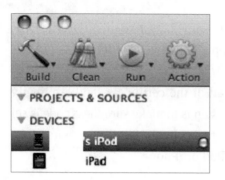

Figure 6.13

Once you are satisfied with your app and ready to sell it, then you will need to follow the instructions online to do so. You'll also need to pay the $99 registration fee for developers.

Uploading your finished app is a relatively simple process. You sign up for your developer account at developer.apple.com, but you upload your app at itunesconnect.apple.com. More than likely you are not already selling music or books on iTunes, but if, by chance, you are, then you will need to get a separate account for each. If you are doing the app as a company, then each company must have a different name on the account; so if, for example, your company's name is Cool Products, and you are already using that name to sell books, then just change it to Cool Products Apps and Apple will not have a problem. You are able to use the same Tax ID or social security number—just not the same name. Before you can proceed with uploading your app, you must fill out all contracts and banking information in iTunesConnect (figure 6.14).

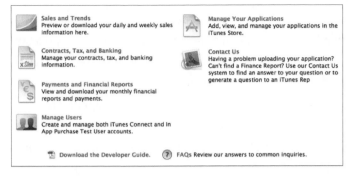

Figure 6.14

In iTunesConnect you will click on "Manage Your Applications" and select "Add New App." The next steps are self-explanatory—just answer the questions about your apps title, description, keywords, category, and add any screenshots. There are really two major ways people will find your app—one, through good marketing; and two, through keywords (i.e., the words or phrases that your app will come up under). Many developers make the mistake of not stepping back to consider keywords people might use to find the app. Let's say, for example, you developed an app for your business, which is a restaurant in Glendale, California; obviously you'll want to include the type of food you have as a keyword, but adding "Glendale California" or "Offbeat Eateries" might also be good choices.

After the application is complete, there's still a few more steps. Once you submit the app, you must first go back into the app by clicking view details, and select "upload binary." It will ask you a couple of questions about encryption—unless your app is using some kind of log-in security, this should not apply to you. Finally, it will say the app is ready to be uploaded and it will refer you to the Application Loader, which is part of the SDK. At this point, you probably will have already received an e-mail alerting you to the fact that they are ready for your upload. The easiest way to find the Application Loader is to go into the Finder and type in "Application Loader"; The physical location of the Loader is under the Developer directory: Developer/Application/Utilities. Again, it will ask you a couple of quick questions about testing the app, then it will ask you to find the location of your binary; once selected you can upload the binary. When it's finished you will get a second e-mail confirming that the binary has been received.

Next . . . you wait! This is the part no developer likes. There's really no way of knowing how long the review process will take; it can be days or weeks. Most developers say it takes about a week to a week and a half. The reason for the delay is, unlike Android, real humans are looking at the app to determine if it's ready for prime time. Mostly they are looking for things like the icon in the application matching the one in the app, but they are also looking for quality applications. Apple has famously said they don't need any more fart apps, and they mean it! Apple is the king of the phones, and they want the best.

As you wait, the best thing to do is start thinking about how you will market the app. It's also never too soon to start thinking about your first update.

In the best-case scenario, your app will be accepted and you will go out and celebrate. But rejections happen. If you develop long enough on Apple, chances are it will happen to you. The key to rejection is to respond creatively.

Creatively? What does that mean? Let me give you a personal example. For several weeks, I had been working with a developer on a study guide app; after all the time investment and testing, we were happy with the end product, and I submitted it to Apple for their review. About a week later, I got the e-mail nobody wants— the rejection. In my case, Apple had declined the app with a cryptic message that apps that were books would be rejected. Huh? You say! If it's an app then it's not a book! I researched the issue on the Internet and found lots of other developers having a similar problem. I took the issue to the Apple review board, and a few days later got a phone call from an Apple employee who told me they were still rejecting my app. I asked what would have to be changed to get them to reconsider and they said to make it not a book! Are you following? Because if you are, then you are one step ahead of me! But I had spent weeks on this app, and I didn't want to just walk away! And so I responded creatively. I made a list of several things that could make it "not a book"—a short quiz, a notepad, a game. I knew Apple wasn't looking for me to create Angry Birds—they just wanted a bit more interactivity—even if they had a funny way of saying it.

In the end, we added a quiz and a note-taking field to the app, and the app was better as a result of the extra effort. I submitted it again, and Apple accepted it in less than twelve hours.

Testing Core Users ▸

Once you have an app ready to go, the final thing to consider is the best way to promote it. For example, people who will use the app are not necessarily the same people who visit the business regularly. How can you promote a service to a group of users whom you might not see on a regular basis?

One way to reach your user base is through a local online campaign. If the business does not have a Facebook page, then it should create one—fan pages regularly attract non-regular business users, or people who want to know what's going on in their community but don't frequently visit the business.

Many businesspeople use smartphones—with this user base, you might collaborate with restaurants and coffeehouses near business areas of the city. Many businesses would be glad to leave out flyers advertising your app, especially if you include their name on the app in a sponsor category or work out some other arrangement. To get people into the business whom you might not usually see, you might put a coupon for a service on the app—all they have to do is show the coupon on their phone.

To publicize your app, you can also look beyond the business at what other businesses have done to get people on their Facebook pages or websites. Many local Chick-fil-A Facebook fan pages, for example, post code words each week on the fan page. If you go to the restaurant on a certain day and say the code word, then you get a reward. People visit the page fanatically to keep up to date just so they don't miss out on something. Thousands of other businesses have similar strategies.

Phones don't have a lot of storage or screen space. So you need to make your app appealing. If customers have to choose between leaving the iPhone app for the Internet Movie Data Base on their phone and the business's app, will they really choose your business's? Why not? As you develop the app, continually ask yourself, "What will make people come back again and again?" For example, why would patrons bother downloading an app that tells them what time the business closes?

Business apps need to be interactive. If it was easy to communicate with customers through an app, and if there are lots of phone-enabled research tools, then the app becomes a more essential tool. If it's not interactive, users will go with other apps every time.

If there is an incentive for patrons to download the app, then you will find users. If not, then you will have wasted a lot of resources. Mobile apps are a bit like animated graphics; when the Internet first became big, every amateur web designer showed off their talents with a flashy animated GIF. Thos GIFs were definitely flashy, but after about three seconds, they became quite annoying. In a nutshell, iPhone apps work in the same way—for every excellent app, there are at least ten apps that fail. Unless your mission in developing an app is to do something cool and flashy and short-lived, then think interactive.

Code for Business App

```html
<HTML>
<head>
<title>Generic Library Logo</title>
<style type="text/css">
.style1 {
text-align: center;
}
.style2 {
text-align: center;
font-size: x-large;
}
.style3 {
margin-right: 0px;
}
</style>
</head>
<body>
<table style="width: 852px; height: 115px">
<tr>
<td class="style2" colspan="3" style="height: 19px"><strong>Generic
Library Logo</strong></td>
</tr>
<tr>
<td class="style1" style="height: 23px; width: 283px"><strong><br />
<img height="90" src="call.jpg" width="65" /><br />
<br />
Call</strong></td>
<td class="style1" style="height: 23px; width: 283px"><br />
<strong><img height="90" src="hours.jpg" width="90" /><br />
<br />
Hours</strong></td>
<td class="style1" style="height: 23px; width: 284px"><strong><br />
<img class="style3" height="86" src="map.jpg" width="94" /><br />
<br />
Locations</strong></td>
</tr>
<tr>
<td class="style1" style="height: 23px; width: 283px"><strong><br />
<img height="88" src="book_catalog.jpg" width="89" /><br />
<br />
Find a Book</strong></td>
<td class="style1" style="height: 23px; width: 283px"><br />
```

```html
<strong><img height="90" src="research.jpg" width="100" /><br />
<br />
Research</strong></td>
<td class="style1" style="height: 23px; width: 284px"><strong><br />
<img class="style3" height="91" src="childrens_services.jpg"
width="75" /><br />
<br />
Children&#39;s Services</strong></td>
</tr>
<tr>
<td class="style1" style="height: 23px; width: 283px"><strong><br />
<img height="103" src="teen.jpg" width="90" /><br />
<br />
Teen Program</strong></td>
<td class="style1" style="height: 23px; width: 283px"><strong><br />
<img height="92" src="computer.jpg" width="100" /><br />
<br />
Computer Classes</strong></td>
<td class="style1" style="height: 23px; width: 284px"><br />
<strong><img height="91" src="text_message.jpg" width="90" /><br />
<br />
Text a Question</strong></td>
</tr>
<tr>
<td class="style1" colspan="3" style="height: 19px"><strong><br />
<img height="50" src="help.jpg" width="54" /><br />
<br />
About</strong></td>
</tr>
</table>
</body>
</html>
```

SEVEN

Beyond the Basics

The point of this book is to make building an app as simple as possible. You can add JavaScript to your app to make it flashier, but talking in detail about JavaScript would take away from the point of this book—keeping it simple.

JavaScript is a pretty powerful language that can do a lot of things, but learning it isn't essential to building a great-looking app. If you know JavaScript, then use it; if you don't, then there's another option: widgets. If you blog or read blogs, then you likely know all about widgets, even if you don't know them by name. Widgets are the small boxes that sit on the sidebars of blogs and offer links to things like Twitter, Facebook, and Google News streams. Widgets appear on the surface to be quite simple, but there are pages of code built into each one. The good news is that you don't have to know the code to build them.

A simple Web search for "widgets" turns up thousands of pages that offer customizable widgets; some are free, and others have small fees attached. You'll need to watch out for widgets that use Flash (which many phones do not currently support—most notably, the iPhone).

Many websites also offer widgets. Twitter is the perfect example. On the Widget web page for Twitter (http://twitter.com/widgets/) you can build a custom widget in just a couple of short steps.

First, on the widget page, select "My Website" (figure 7.1).

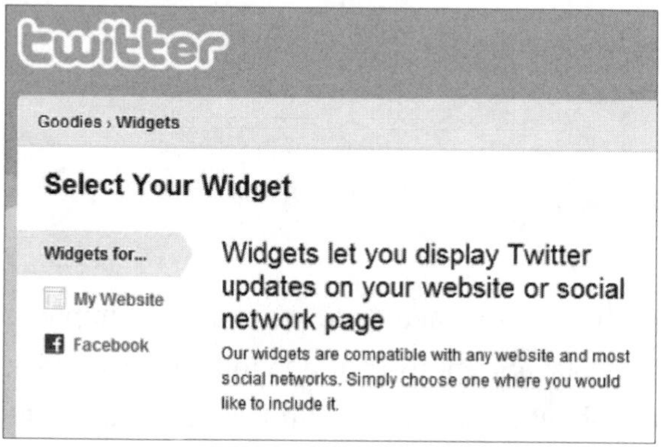

Figure 7.1

On the following page you will see several options; choose "Profile Widget," which will display your business's most recent tweets.

Next you can customize your widget (figure 7.2). Under the user name, you ideally would put the name of your business, but you can also put authors, important businesspeople, or the name of anyone else with a public Twitter account. This would give your app content if you don't have time to do it yourself. @chickfila is a business that uses Twitter to send out coupons and interact with its customers. Customers love coupons, but it's also a nice feeling when you see that the company actually reads what its customers are saying and lets them know that it cares. Many airlines, such as JetBlue, have used Twitter to account for their mistakes, apologize publicly to their customers, let them know they are truly working to solve the problem, and turn bad PR into good PR.

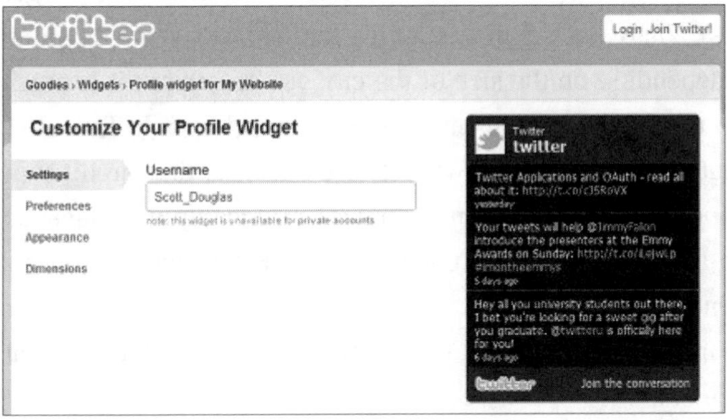

Figure 7.2

Under "Preferences," you can select how many tweets you display. Although the limit on Twitter is thirty tweets, it is advisable to consider the screen size of the mobile device you are developing for. You don't want users to have to scroll too much—ideally, you don't want them to scroll at all. Because of that, you might keep the number of tweets displayed to four.

Under "Appearance," make sure the colors you select match the colors of your app. Under "Dimensions," you can adjust them to the dimensions of the phone or choose "auto width" if you want it to resize the widget yourself.

Finally, go to the bottom of the page and select "Finish & Grab Code" (figure 7.3). Now just copy the code and paste it into your app's code.

Figure 7.3

If you are thinking about providing a chat-based reference service (if you are not, you should be—by not doing so, you'll miss an entire generation of users), then consider LibraryH3lp (http://libraryh3lp.com). It was started by librarians for librarians, but they also work with businesses (and at a fraction of the cost of larger vendors). There is a small annual fee for the site's service (which varies depending on the size of the city you're in), but it is much cheaper than many similar services. Meebo and Google Talk offer free chat services, but their widgets use Flash, so they aren't supported on the iPhone app. In contrast, LibraryH3lp uses Java, so it's app-friendly. The source code of LibraryH3lp's widget appears at the end of this chapter.

In a mobile browser, that code from box 4 would look similar to figure 7.4.

It is worth noting that chat is not something you want to have if you don't plan to have someone in charge of monitoring it. Most chat services allow you to receive e-mail alerts when a person has entered the chat, so people don't have to be glued to the screen waiting for it; but, just like a phone, when the chat rings, you want to answer it immediately.

Widgetbox (www.widgetbox .com) is one of the most popular widget builders; it's free but advertisement-supported. A pro version (without the ads) is also available, starting at $29.99 a year. The site offers both Flash- and Java-based widgets.

Facebook also provides steps for embedding profiles into websites (http://developers.facebook.com/

Figure 7.4

docs/guides/web/). Widgetbox, however, makes a much more user-friendly version, and if you are new to development, it is the better choice. Just make sure you copy the Java-based version of the widget and not the Flash-based one.

Widgetbox also makes it easy to develop a mobile app (www .widgetbox.com/mobile/). If you want a basic mobile web app (not a native app) that shows Twitter, Facebook, or Flickr updates, then Widgetbox might work well for the business; it does not, however, allow for users to edit the source code, and you might quickly find it to be too restrictive for your business.

Widgipedia (www.widgipedia.com) is another great resource for finding widgets; however, they are user-submitted and customizable.

PhoneGap offers several codes that developers can copy for use in their own app; you can find these in the Community section of the website (www.phonegap.com/community/). It's frequently updated, so check back often. A useful code is for including a map, based on the phone's GPS (http://docs.phonegap.com/en/1.0.0/ phonegap_geolocation_geolocation.md.html).

I have tested all of the widgets and tools in this chapter to ensure that they will work with an iPhone app. As I have said before, however, JavaScript is tricky on mobile web apps and native apps, so always test before implementing. For every JavaScript that I have tested successfully on a native iPhone app, a dozen more come back with errors.

Code for Library H3lp's Widget

```html
<html xmlns="http://www.w3.org/1999/xhtml" xml:lang="en"
lang="en">
 <head>
 <meta http-equiv=content-type content="text/html; charset=UTF-8">
 <meta name="viewport" content="width=device-width,
initial-scale=1.0 user-scalable=yes" />
 <title></title>
 <link type="text/css" rel="stylesheet" href="/css/mobile.css" />

 <style id="dynamic" type="text/css">
 </style>
 <script type="text/javascript" src="http://ajax.googleapis.com/ajax/
libs/jquery/1.3.2/jquery.min.js"></script>
 <script type="text/javascript" src="http://d1aaqh87bn7fin.cloudfront
.net/mobile_2010011801.min.js"></script>
 <!—
 <script type="text/javascript" src="/js/lib/strophe.js"></script>
 <script type="text/javascript" src="/emoticons/emoticons
.js"></script>
 <script type="text/javascript" src="/js/mobile.js"></script>
 —>
 </head>
 <body>
 <div id="header">
 <img id="presence" src="/presence/image/simpletext/unavailable" />
 <h1 id="title"></h1>
 </div>
 <div id="to" jid="my-queue@chat.libraryh3lp.com" lang="en"></div>
 <div id="recv"></div>
 <div id="send">
 <form action="#" method="post" onSubmit="return false;">
 <textarea id="msg">chat requires javascript...
 </textarea>
 </form>
 <div id="buttons"><a href="#" onclick="libraryh3lp.sendLine(); return
false;"><img height="42" width="30" src="/images/mobilesend.png"
/></a></div>
 </div>
 <div id="status"><a id="mail" href="#" onclick="libraryh3lp
.mailTranscript(); return false;">Email transcript
 </a></div>
 </body>
</html>
```

EIGHT

Other Ways to Go Mobile

The point of this book is to show businesses how simple it can be to develop mobile applications. For the most part, mobile apps run on smartphones. However, businesses can also proactively investigate other mobile application programming interfaces (APIs).

Foursquare (for documentation information, see http://groups .google.com/group/foursquare-api/web/api-documentation/), which some bill as the next Twitter, is a location-based social media app that allows people to tell their friends exactly where they are and become "mayors" of locations they visit frequently. Gowalla (http://gowalla.com) is another social website like Foursquare that's growing in popularity; unlike Foursquare, though, Gowalla offers a little more in terms of customization.

When thinking about mobile apps, businesses should think of as many free technologies as possible for promotion—Foursquare and Yelp already have apps that you can easily link to. If your business has not staked its claim on Foursquare, why not? It's a perfect avenue for promotion: people can check into the business with the business app and get something for free—it can be something as simple as a cup of coffee or donut; you don't have to (or want to) break the bank with this—you just want something that makes the customer feel special.

Some of the best social media sites that work on mobile phones are the same ones that are most popular on the Web: Facebook, Twitter, YouTube, and Flickr. If your business doesn't have a Facebook fan page, it's time. This is true too, though to a lesser extent, with the other three. What better way to showcase your business than with videos and photos? What's great about all the social media sites is that they are integrated together—you can feed Twitter updates into Facebook and share YouTube videos and Flickr slideshows instantly on Twitter and Facebook. The best thing about these sites, however, is that you don't have to do anything to go mobile. If you have a page on Twitter or Facebook, it's already mobile-compatible—no extra steps are required.

Business apps don't need to do something never done before—they just need to take what has been done and apply it to their own business. Save yourself time and trouble by finding code that's already finished. Look at companies that have done it right and just copy their model and make it your own. I hope you decide to develop a mobile app, but at the very least, I hope you make sure that your business is actively involved in the mobile technologies mentioned here.

WYSIWYG App Editors ▶ ···

Mobile app development is a powerful business tool that every business should try out in some capacity, but not every business will have the time or resources to make it happen. For this reason, it's worth noting some alternate solutions. The disadvantage of using the alternates is their cost, and in most cases, the limited ability they offer to customize apps. Their advantages are that they will help you set up much quicker and nearly guarantee that your app will make it into an app store.

Some of the tools listed here will basically build an app for you; others provide an easy WYSIWYG interface. All are available for the iPhone; most are available for Android; some are available for BlackBerry and other mobile devices.

The up-front costs of these interfaces can be expensive, but the cost is next to nothing compared with what you would pay a programmer to take on the project.

Appanda

Website: www.appanda.com

Platform: Do-it-yourself (DIY) app solution for iPhone and Android

Summary: Appanda is best for businesses that want to feature only iPhone and/or Android versions of already existing content (e.g., feeding in a blog or a video hosted on YouTube).

Pricing: $29.99 per month plus a one-time activation fee of $99

Swebapps

Website: www.swebapps.com

Platform: iPhone

Summary: The interface is a bit more visually appealing than some do-it-yourself apps that feature a boxier look.

Swebapps has all the same features as other DIY builders but also incorporates tools to create forms, lists, maps, and events pages.

Pricing: Basic plan starts at $29 a month, plus a $399 one-time fee

AppBreeder

Website: www.appbreeder.com

Platform: iPhone and web app

Summary: There are no up-front fees, but the site is limited in terms of customization and has a very generic look.

Pricing: $29–49 per month for iPhone app or free web app

My App Builder

Website: www.myappbuilder.com

Platform: iPhone and Android

Summary: There are no up-front fees, but the website offers few screenshots and few details about features.

Pricing: $29 per month

Build an App

Website: www.buildanapp.com

Platform: BlackBerry, Android, Windows Mobile, Mobile Web, iPhone

Summary: Available on more devices than most app builders, and for a price that is cheaper than most, but the app has a very generic look and is limited in terms of customization.

Pricing: $14 a month and $19 set-up fee for all apps, but
iPhone app requires $199 set-up fee

Mobile App Loader

Website: www.mobileapploader.com

Platform: iPhone, iPad, and Android

Summary: This is not the best-looking app builder, but it has
low fees and is one of a few compatible with the iPad.
Don't let the price fool you, however; extra buttons and
features incur additional fees. There is also not a lot of
room for customization.

Pricing: $4.99 per month and $59.99 set-up fee

Google App Inventor ▶

Things were more complex for app developers just a few years
ago—PhoneGap certainly has helped take away the complexity of
mobile app development. In the past year, dozens of virtual companies have emerged promising to assist users who want to go mobile
but lack programming skills. In this section I discuss Google's App
Inventor (http://appinventor.googlelabs.com).

In my experience, developing apps for the iPhone is much
simpler than developing for Android; Apple has spent much more
money on app development, and it's obvious in its presentation and
SDK functionality. Google is still playing catch-up. If you want
to develop an app using PhoneGap, then refer to the appendix,
which gives a list of where to go for tutorials on the Web. Google
App Inventor, however, is entirely different from the traditional
method of app development, so it's worth noting here what it is
and how it works.

App Inventor was first made available on July 12, 2010; the tool claims to be so easy that elementary school children can use it with little effort. The interface uses drag-and-drop objects to create apps that run on any Android phone.

Because of App Inventor's simplicity, it is difficult to develop an app that is visually stunning. It is, however, an excellent place to test mobile development and decide what the best practices for the business will be. As Google continues to improve the drag-and-drop developer, it will most definitely get easier to use and more powerful.

At the time of writing, Google App Inventor has only recently become public; Google is rapidly updating the program and some instructions here will likely already be outdated.

Is it simple to use? App Inventor takes some getting used to, but it's much simpler than developing a native iPhone app. Is it cool? Not so much, but it has promise. I suspect that it will continue to get better—app development is something that Google has emphasized in recent months.

When Google first tested App Inventor, it used elementary-age kids to see if it was easy enough for them to use. It was. So can you develop an app quickly through the inventor? Yes. Should you? Probably not yet.

What follows is a very brief look at how the App Inventor works. It's still being updated, and it will likely look more polished in coming months when it becomes more public. As with any rapidly growing technology, what you see here will most likely not be what you see by the time this book is printed.

If you use Google Docs, then the App Inventor interface will look a little bit familiar. When you sign in, the first thing you will see is a list of all your current projects (if you have any) (figure 8.1). In the menu, you can either click on "New" to open a new project or on "More Actions" to download the code of previously built projects.

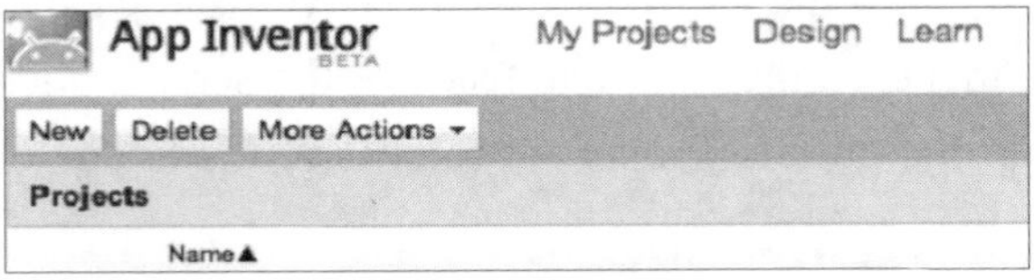

Figure 8.1

Next you need to name the project; make sure you do not include spaces in the name (figure 8.2).

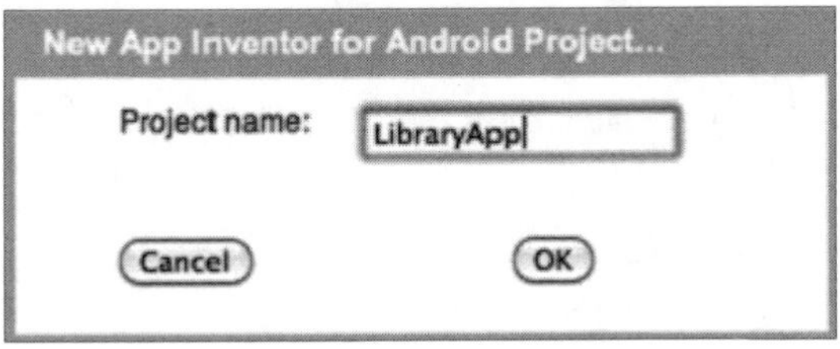

Figure 8.2

Then the project interface appears (figure 8.3). The first thing you will probably notice is how visual it is; this is because of its drag-and-drop interface.

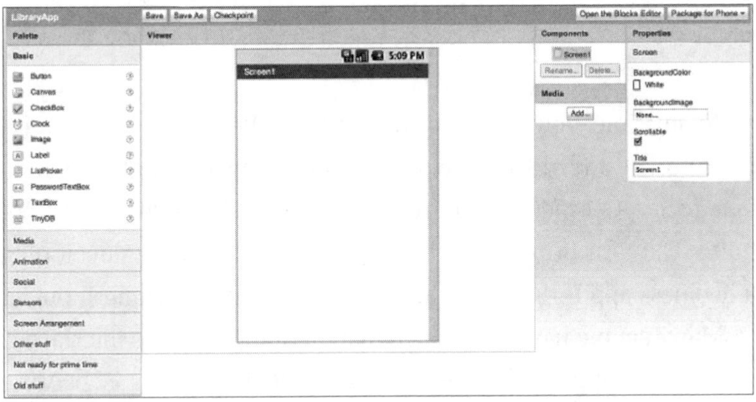

Figure 8.3

If you want to include an image, then you can simply click "Image" in the Palette menu on the left-hand side of the screen and drop the image into the viewer. From there, you can go into the Components menu on the right-hand side of the screen, click on "Image," and then go into Properties to change the image or rename it (figure 8.4).

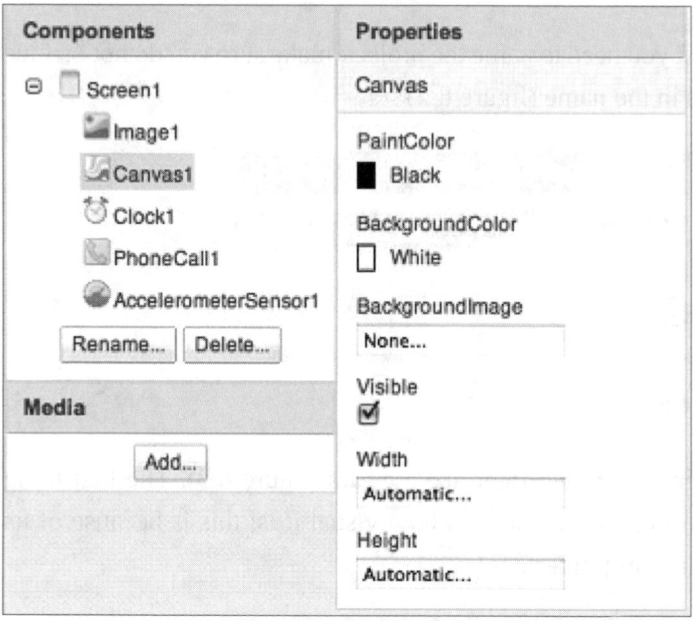

Components	Properties
⊖ ☐ Screen1	Canvas
🖼 Image1	PaintColor
🎨 Canvas1	■ Black
⏱ Clock1	BackgroundColor
📞 PhoneCall1	☐ White
🔘 AccelerometerSensor1	BackgroundImage
Rename... Delete...	None...
Media	Visible ☑
Add...	Width
	Automatic...
	Height
	Automatic...

Figure 8.4

At any time, you can click on "Learn" at the top of the screen for full tutorials and videos; the project, like many at Google, is still in beta form. As I mentioned, from a commercial standpoint, it's not quite ready for prime time, but if you are considering developing a business app for Android, it's certainly worth checking it out.

Many people have speculated that this simple-to-use interface is the future of app development. One can only hope that it is, because it's certainly a step in the right direction.

Appendix

The following is a list of where to go for tutorials on the Web if you want to develop an app using PhoneGap:

iPhone: http://phonegap.pbworks.com/Getting-Started-with
-PhoneGap-(iPhone)

Android: http://phonegap.pbworks.com/Getting-started-with
-Android-PhoneGap-in-Eclipse

BlackBerry: http://phonegap.pbworks.com/Getting-Started
-with-PhoneGap-(BlackBerry)

Palm: http://phonegap.pbworks.com/Getting-Started-with
-PhoneGap-Palm

Windows Mobile: http://phonegap.pbworks.com/Getting
-Started-with-PhoneGap-(WiMo)

Appendix

Glossary

3G Stands for third-generation mobile telecommunications; this technology gives users the ability to access the Internet through their phone wirelessly. Speed varies from 1 MPS (megabits per second) to 4 MPS; Apple recently announced 3G capable of 12 MPS. The speed varies depending on location and cellular provider.

4G In theory, 4G is the next generation up from 3G. In practice, 4G often has comparable speeds to 3G. Several speed tests, for example, have showed that the AT&T 3G iPhone is faster than T-Mobile's 4G Galaxy. Many see 4G as more of a selling tactic; the next generation of data speed is HSDPA+ (High-Speed Downlink Packet Access), which will be capable of 42 MPS and eventually 150 MPS in the more distant future.

Absolute Positioning Absolute positioning is when you put an object (such as an image) in a specified place (as opposed to floating or relative positioning).

Accelerometer   Nearly all smartphones have accelerometers built in; this allows the phone to know when it is being turned and change the screen from horizontal to landscape.

Android   The phone operating system developed by Google; it is one of the most popular smartphone operating systems and is also the basis for several tablets and eReaders (including the Galaxy, Kindle Fire, Nook, and Xoom).

API   Stands for application programming interface; the code for API is often freely distributed online and can be copied and expanded upon.

CSS   Stands for Cascading Style Sheet; CSS makes it easy to create a style for a web page, so the user doesn't have to keep rewriting the code—the CSS might, for instance, say all web pages have a size-12 font and the color green.

Debug   Debugging is most often the final step of any kind of programming; this is where the user will test the code or program to make sure there are no errors.

Domain   Domains are where websites are hosted—the domain address is the same as the web address.

Flash   Flash is the multimedia platform developed by Adobe to show animation, video, and other interactive content. Apple has continually insisted that Flash slows down the performance and battery life of phones, and has refused to support it on the iPhone.

Floating Image   Contrary to relative and absolute positioning images, floating images have no position.

Geolocation   Geolocation is when an app uses the phone's GPS to find the user's position; Yelp, for instance, uses this feature to recommend restaurants in the nearby area.

GIF   Stands for Graphics Interchange Format. GIF is an image format that is often used on banners because its file size can be compressed to a smaller size.

JavaScript   JavaScript is a programming language used to add interactive features to a website.

JPEG   JPEG is one of the most common picture formats because it can compress photos with very little quality loss.

Open Source   Open source is freely distributed software that can be copied and redistributed.

OS   Stands for operating system; this is the platform that the software runs—Microsoft Windows OS is the best example of an operating system.

PHP   Stands for Hypertext Preprocessor; in mobile development, PHP is used to create software within an app.

Pixels   Pixels are the amount of resolution inside a photo.

Relative Positioning   Relative positioning moves an object (or image) to its position based on how it relates to another object.

SDK   Stands for software development kit; this is the software that iPhone, Android, Windows, and so on give programmers to develop apps for their system.

SQL   Stands for Structured Query Language. SQL is used to build a database within an app.

WML   Stands for Wireless Markup Language; this enables cell phones to display websites.

Xcode   Program created by Apple to allow programmers to develop apps for the iPhone.

Index

source codes
    business apps, 70–71
    Library H3lp's widget, 76
staff training, 10–12
StatCounter, 10
Survey on the Spot, 11
surveying users, 9–10
SurveyMonkey, 11
Swebapps (website), 81–82

T

tables versus CSS, 28
Tally Counter, 12
Tallymander, 12
testing core users, 67–69
text editor, CSS and, 30
texting services (native app
    element), 55
Thomson, Laura, 49
training staff, 10–12
Twitter (website), 79

U

users, surveying, 9–10

V

vibration (PhoneGap feature),
    45–46
videos button (native app
    element), 55

W

WCSS (wireless CSS), 24–25
web languages, 7–8
website accessibility, 19
website layout considerations,
    31–32
Welling, Luke, 49
Widgetbox, 76–77
widgets for mobile apps, 73–78
Widgipedia (website), 77a
Wireless CSS (WCSS), 2, 24
Wireless Markup Language
    (WML), 7–8
World Conference on Soft
    Computing (WSC3), 21
WYSIWYG app editors, 2–3, 21,
    80–83

X

Xcode, 58
Xcode Organizer, 62
XHTML-MP, 2

Senior High School Library
Chippewa Falls, Wisconsin

Senior High School Library
Chippewa Falls, Wisconsin